MARIE CURIE
ADVANCES THE STUDY OF RADIOACTIVITY

by Rebecca Rowell

Content Consultant
Peter Soppelsa
Assistant Professor
Department of the History of Science
The University of Oklahoma

Core Library

An Imprint of Abdo Publishing
abdopublishing.com

abdopublishing.com

Published by Abdo Publishing, a division of ABDO, PO Box 398166, Minneapolis, Minnesota 55439. Copyright © 2016 by Abdo Consulting Group, Inc. International copyrights reserved in all countries. No part of this book may be reproduced in any form without written permission from the publisher. Core Library™ is a trademark and logo of Abdo Publishing.

Printed in the United States of America, North Mankato, Minnesota
072015
012016

Cover Photo: Bettmann/Corbis
Interior Photos: Bettmann/Corbis, 1, 28; Culture Club/Getty Images, 4, 45; Oxford Science Archive/Print Collector/Getty Images, 6, 27; Alexander Bedrin/iStockphoto, 10; Red Line Editorial/iStockphoto, 13; Universal History Archive/Getty Images, 16, 22, 35; The LIFE Picture Collection/Getty Images, 19; SSPL/Getty Images, 20; Willis D. Vaughn/National Geographic/ Getty Images, 24; John B. Carnett/Bonnier Corp./Getty Images, 32; Red Line Editorial, 37; Patrick Kovarik/AFP/Getty Images, 39; Michael Utech/iStockphoto, 40

Editor: Arnold Ringstad
Series Designer: Maggie Villaume

Library of Congress Control Number: 2015945762

Cataloging-in-Publication Data
Rowell, Rebecca.
 Marie Curie advances the study of radioactivity / Rebecca Rowell.
   p. cm. -- (Great moments in science)
 ISBN 978-1-68078-018-5 (lib. bdg.)
 Includes bibliographical references and index.
 1. Chemists--France--Juvenile literature. 2. Women chemists--France--Juvenile literature. 3. Physicists--France--Juvenile literature. 4. Women physicists--France--Juvenile literature. 5. Radioactivity--History--Juvenile literature.
 I. Title.
 540--dc23
                                                                    2015945762

CONTENTS

PRIZE-WINNING RESEARCH

Marie Curie sat at the Royal Institute in London, England. The Polish-born resident of France was a brilliant scientist. She watched as her husband, Pierre, gave a lecture. It was June 1903. As a woman, Marie was not allowed to present her work. Instead, she listened as Pierre talked about their shared research.

Marie and Pierre Curie worked together to study radiation and its effects.

The Curies' daughter Irene was born in 1897.

The Royal Society had invited the couple. This scientific group held a popular lecture series. The theater was packed. Marie sat in the front row. The Curies were famous for their work with radium. They had discovered this element in 1898.

Pierre's talk included a demonstration. He showed how radium glowed. He showed how it could affect other objects. Radium released invisible energy. Pierre showed the audience his arm. It was burned from touching radium. He told the crowd radium might be used to treat cancer. He showed it could damage healthy tissue in a body. He hoped it could do the same to unhealthy tissue.

Choosing Radioactivity

The Curies' work with radium went back several years. It began with Marie's college research. Marie enrolled at the Sorbonne in 1891. This school is in Paris, France. It was one of the world's first universities. Marie studied physics and math. She earned master's degrees in both subjects.

In 1894 Marie was looking for a place to do her research. Pierre Curie offered space in his laboratory. The two shared an interest in science. They soon fell in love and married.

Marie next wanted to earn a doctoral degree. First she needed a topic to study. She had learned some elements gave off invisible energy. She decided to study it. When Marie began her work, this energy did not have a name. She eventually named it herself. She called it radioactivity.

The Davy Medal

After Pierre's lecture, the Royal Society gave the Curies the Davy Medal. This award is named for English scientist Humphry Davy. It honors important work in chemistry. The Curies won it for their work with radium.

A New Era

The week after the 1903 talk in London, Marie completed her doctoral degree. Later that year, the Curies received the Nobel Prize in physics. This award is given by a Swedish committee. At first the committee did not plan to give it to Marie. They planned to give the award only to Pierre and a fellow scientist, Henri Becquerel. But Pierre made it clear that Marie had to be included. She had carried out important work in the study of radium.

The committee members changed their minds and awarded the prize to all three scientists. Marie became the first woman to receive a Nobel Prize. She showed that women were as capable as men at scientific research. Her work helped launch a new field of physics. She became one of the most important scientists in history.

FURTHER EVIDENCE

Chapter One discusses reactions to the Curie's work. What is one of the main points of this chapter? What are some pieces of evidence that support this point? Visit the website below. Does the information on the website support the chapter's point? Does it add new evidence?

Nobel Prize: Marie Curie
mycorelibrary.com/radioactivity

CHAPTER TWO

ATOMS AND RADIATION

Marie Curie was a physicist. Physics involves the study of matter. Matter makes up everything humans can see, touch, or detect. Physicists examine what matter is made of. They also study how it interacts with other matter. Some physicists look at huge things, such as stars and galaxies. Others study tiny objects, such as atoms.

All matter is made up of atoms.

Discovering Particles

Protons, neutrons, and electrons were discovered within a few decades of each other in the late 1800s and early 1900s. Joseph Thompson discovered electrons. Ernest Rutherford discovered protons in 1919. Finally, James Chadwick discovered neutrons in 1932.

Elements and Atoms

Atoms are the basic building blocks of matter. Atoms contain three types of particles. These are protons, neutrons, and electrons. Protons have a positive charge. Neutrons have no charge. Electrons have a negative charge. Protons and neutrons make up the nucleus. This is the center of an atom. Electrons move around the nucleus.

The number of protons in an atom determines what kind of element it is. For example, a hydrogen atom always has one proton. An atom of gold has 79 protons. An atom of radium has 88 protons. There are more than 100 elements. Each has unique properties.

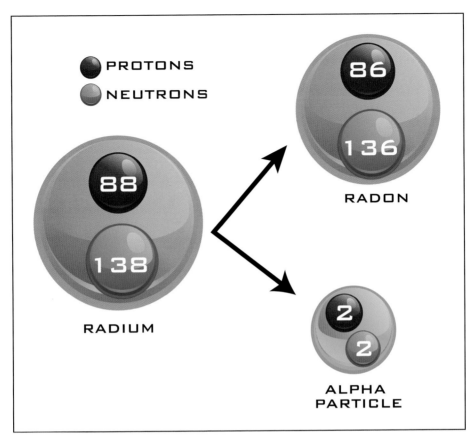

The Decay of Radium

This diagram shows an atom of radium and its radioactive decay. The original radium atom has 88 protons and 138 neutrons. It gives off an alpha particle. This consists of two protons and two neutrons. The result is an atom with 86 protons, the element radon. How does this diagram help you better understand the process of radioactive decay?

Radiation and Radioactivity

Some elements are radioactive. They gradually give off particles and energy. When they end up with fewer protons, they become other elements. The energy released in this process is called radiation. Only three radioactive elements occur naturally. They are radium, thorium, and uranium.

Radiation moves through air, liquids, and solids invisibly. It can change the matter it encounters. If it strikes living tissue, it can damage it. Sometimes tissue recovers. Other times it cannot. Radiation can burn skin and cause hair loss or even cancer.

It is possible to defend against radiation. A sheet of paper can block some types of radiation. Other types can be blocked by a thin piece of metal. The most damaging types of radiation require more protection. Thick layers of earth, concrete, or metal are needed. Marie Curie did not know the dangers of radiation. She suffered terribly after years of exposure to it.

CHAPTER THREE

FROM POLAND TO PARIS

Marie Curie was born on November 7, 1867, in Warsaw, Poland. Her birth name was Maria Sklodowska. She was the youngest of five children. Maria was an excellent student. She graduated from high school at age 15. She later worked as a governess to support her sister Bronya.

Marie, left, helped support her sister Bronya, right.

In 1891, 23-year-old Maria enrolled at the Sorbonne. She used the French version of her name, Marie. She was far behind her classmates, but she worked hard to change that. She earned two master's degrees by 1894.

Advances in Physics

Scientists made significant advances in the 1890s. In November 1895, German physicist Wilhelm Conrad Röntgen discovered something strange. He sent electricity through a tube pointed at crystals. The crystals glowed. They continued glowing even when he blocked the tube's light. Röntgen realized invisible energy was causing the crystals to glow. This energy passed through

Magnetism and Love

In spring 1894, an organization hired Marie to study the magnetism of steel. Marie told a Polish physicist she needed a place to do her work. The man introduced Marie to Pierre Curie. Pierre was a professor who studied magnetism. The couple worked together. They soon fell in love. They married in July 1895.

Röntgen's work paved the way for later discoveries in radiation.

solid objects. He called the rays of mysterious energy X-rays. Two weeks later, he used X-rays to create a photograph of his wife's hand. The rays traveled through her flesh, revealing her bones in the image.

In January 1896, French physicist Henri Becquerel built on Röntgen's research. He focused on the element uranium. Becquerel placed a glass plate in a drawer. The plate had a light-sensitive coating. He put

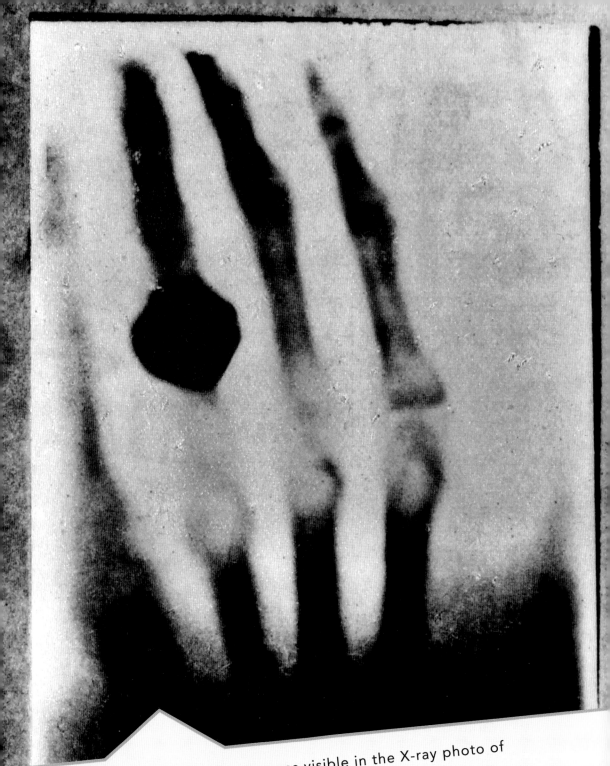

Röntgen's wife's ring was visible in the X-ray photo of her hand.

a sample of uranium on the plate. Then he shut the drawer. Even away from sunlight, the uranium left a mark. This meant the uranium gave off its own energy. Becquerel had observed natural radioactivity.

Most scientists did not recognize the importance of Becquerel's work. They believed he simply saw a type of X-ray. Becquerel later lost interest in his research. Marie decided to investigate the energy he had discovered.

Studying Radioactivity

Marie began her doctoral studies in 1897. Her laboratory was at the school where Pierre worked. She used a device called an electrometer. Pierre and his brother had invented it. It could measure very low amounts of electricity.

Marie used the tool to measure air exposed to uranium. Her goal was to examine how well the air conducted electricity. She studied several samples of uranium. Some samples were wet. Others were dry. Some were solid chunks. Others were ground-up

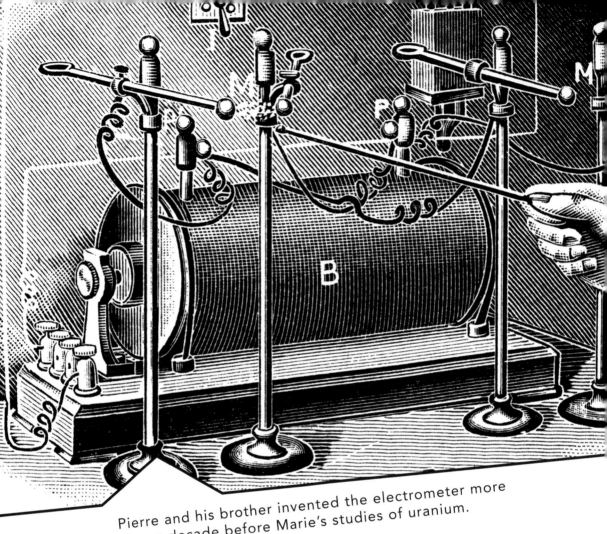

Pierre and his brother invented the electrometer more than a decade before Marie's studies of uranium.

powders. In every test, the uranium had the same electrical effect. This showed the element's physical condition didn't make a difference. The rays were a result of the uranium's atoms.

Marie expanded her research beyond uranium. Perhaps other matter produced rays. Marie tested all known elements. In April 1898, she found that thorium also released rays. Marie coined the term *radioactivity* to describe this energy.

Marie continued investigating radioactivity. She examined minerals, which can contain many different elements. One mineral she studied was called pitchblende. It showed more radioactivity than any individual element. Marie knew something unknown was giving off the extra radiation. She was determined to find the cause. Her work would change the history of science.

PERSPECTIVES
Marie's Hypothesis about Atoms

Marie believed uranium's rays came from its atoms. She thought these atoms contained or released radiation. Her hypothesis was a new idea in science. At the time, researchers believed the atom was the smallest piece of a material. Marie's ideas about radiation would require even smaller particles that made up each atom.

CHAPTER FOUR

DISCOVERING NEW ELEMENTS

Marie worked to uncover the secret of pitchblende. She decided to separate the different parts of the mineral. That way she could isolate whatever was giving off radiation.

Discovering Elements

Marie and Pierre began separating pitchblende. French chemist Gustave Bémont helped them. The

Pitchblende is still mined today.

three scientists began work on April 14, 1898. They poured chemicals on pitchblende to remove elements. Then they studied the remaining material. On June 27, Marie measured radioactivity 300 times that of uranium. Three weeks later, Pierre recorded even higher readings.

Eventually, Marie and Pierre isolated the radioactive material. It was similar to the element bismuth. However, they knew bismuth was not radioactive. Their material

Separating the parts of pitchblende was a complicated process.

Samples of radium glowed in the dark.

was a new element. Marie and Pierre announced their discovery in July 1898. They named the new element polonium after Poland, Marie's homeland.

Later that year, in December, the couple announced the discovery of another new element in pitchblende. They named it radium. The name came from the Latin word *radius*, which means "ray."

Isolating Radium

The Curies discovered polonium and radium using electrical measurements. Their study relied on data from invisible rays. But skeptical scientists wanted physical proof. Marie set to work gathering a visible sample of radium to satisfy these doubters. In 1899 Austria's government provided her with 220 pounds (100 kg) of pitchblende. Marie used several techniques to separate it. She boiled, filtered, and grinded it. Finally she was able to provide proof. She presented 0.003 ounces (0.1 g) of radium.

Marie and Pierre's work made them celebrities. They became very popular. Marie earned more fame

Processing Pitchblende

Marie and Pierre partnered with a chemical company in 1899. It created a new method for processing pitchblende. The company did the initial work of physically separating parts of the pitchblende. Once this was done, Marie would take over.

on July 25, 1903. She became the first woman in France to earn a doctoral degree. She then became the first woman to receive a Nobel Prize.

The next year, she wrote about her research in an American magazine. The article sparked more interest in radium. But Marie's life would soon change. Her work with radiation would take her life in new directions.

Marie wrote about her work with radium in her laboratory, an old, abandoned shed that was far from comfortable:

> *Yet it was in this miserable old shed that we passed the best and happiest years of our life, devoting our entire days to our work. Often I had to prepare our lunch in the shed, so as not to interrupt some particularly important operation. Sometimes I had to spend a whole day mixing a boiling mass with a heavy iron rod nearly as large as myself. I would be broken with fatigue at the day's end. Other days, on the contrary, the work would be a most minute and delicate fractional crystallization, in the effort to concentrate the radium. . . . But I shall never be able to express the joy of the untroubled quietness of this atmosphere of research and the excitement of actual progress with the confident hope of still better results.*

> *Source: "In Her Own Words: The Struggle to Isolate Radium." Marie Curie. American Institute of Physics, 2015. Web. May 14, 2015.*

What's the Big Idea?

Take a close look at this description Marie wrote about her radium research. What is she trying to say about her experience? What were the challenges? What were the rewards? Pick out two details she uses to make her point.

RADIONE
STRENGTH OF IRON
ENERGY OF RADIUM
RADIONE
PRODUCTS CORPORATION
NEW YORK CITY

RADIATION USES

The Curies' discovery of radium, which glowed blue, set a new industry into motion. Radium became a fad. Companies painted wristwatch faces with radium to make them glow in the dark. The cosmetics industry advertised radium lotions it said would make skin healthier. Many people thought radium was some sort of wonder drug. These claims were mostly untrue.

Tablets containing radium were among many fake medical treatments produced with radioactive materials.

However, there were some legitimate uses for medical radiation. X-rays had already proven useful. Pierre's self-experiments prompted doctors to use the substance to fight cancer. In 1904 a French factory began working with the Curies to make radium available for medical use. However, Pierre's work with radioactivity was cut short when he died suddenly in 1906. Marie lost her love and her research partner. But she did not lose her passion for radioactivity.

The Radium Institute

Marie set to work establishing the Radium

Life after Pierre

Pierre Curie died in an accident on April 19, 1906. A horse-drawn cart struck him as he crossed a street. After his death, Marie renewed her focus on her work. On May 13, 1906, Marie took over Pierre's post at the Sorbonne. She was the first woman to teach there. In 1910 Marie published *Treatise on Radioactivity*. The following year, she received a second Nobel Prize for her work with radioactivity. This time the award was in the field of chemistry. The honor made her the only woman to receive a Nobel Prize in two fields.

The Radium Institute became an important site of radiation research.

Institute. This organization would be dedicated to the study of radioactivity. After getting funding, Marie was able to hire researchers and build a research facility. The institute was ready in 1914. That year, war broke out in Europe. It would get Marie working with radioactivity in a new way.

Marie used X-rays to help wounded soldiers during World War I (1914–1918). X-rays allowed medical workers to find bullets inside bodies.

This made it easier for surgeons to remove them. Marie's efforts led to the construction of radiology vehicles. These cars had built-in X-ray machines that could be used in the field.

Marie learned how to drive and how to operate the X-ray equipment. She also took anatomy courses. She enlisted her daughter, 17-year-old Irène, as an assistant. In fall 1914, the pair made their first journey to the front to take X-rays. Marie also helped train approximately 150 women to use X-ray machines. These workers conducted more than 1 million exams.

Today medical professionals continue to rely on X-rays to help patients. Doctors use X-rays to see broken bones and diagnose medical issues. Dentists use X-rays to identify cavities and other dental problems.

Harmful Effects

In the 1920s, the dangers of radiation became evident. People who worked with radium became sick. Some researchers died at young ages. Uranium

0.01 mSv	increased chance of cancer
100 mSv	radiation poisoning
700 mSv	vomiting
1,000 mSv	itching, nausea
4,000 mSv	infection of lymph nodes, hair loss
8,000 mSv	impaired thinking, bone damage
20,000 mSv	damage to intestines
80,000 mSv	instant death

Radiation's Effects on the Body

This chart shows the effects of radiation on the body at different doses. The dose is measured in millisieverts (mSv), named for Swedish radiation researcher Rolf Maximilian Sievert. A chest X-ray results in a dose of about 0.04 millisieverts. How does the chart help you better understand the dangers of high radiation doses?

miners suffered from lung cancer. A group of women who brushed radium paint on watch faces became ill. They were known as the Radium Girls.

Discovering Artificial Radioactivity

Marie Curie's interest in science continued with her daughter Irène. Like her mother, Irène fell in love with and married a researcher. His name was Frédéric Joliot. The couple worked in Marie's lab at the Radium Institute. They advanced the study of radioactivity. In early 1934, they discovered a method for making materials radioactive. The couple received a Nobel Prize in chemistry in 1935 for this work.

Marie also suffered from the effects of radiation. In 1920 a doctor diagnosed her with cataracts. Surgeries improved her eyesight, but with time Marie's health continued worsening. One day in May 1934, she left her lab early because she was not feeling well. Doctors could not agree on what was ailing Marie. Finally a Swiss physician told her she had an incurable blood disorder. Her work with radiation had made her sick. Marie never returned to the lab. She died on July 4, 1934.

The caskets of Marie and Pierre were displayed to the public and honored in 1995.

Radiation and Radioactivity Today

Marie's discoveries remain an important part of everyday life. From medical diagnoses and treatments to power from nuclear plants, radiation has benefitted the world. At the same time, Marie's death showed the world the dangers of radiation. Radioactive

Nuclear power plants provide power to millions of people.

pollution from nuclear weapons and power plant waste have also shown how deadly radiation can be.

Marie's study of radioactivity changed the fields of physics and chemistry forever. Her passion for research and her powerful insights made her a trailblazer. She remains a household name and an inspiration to future scientists.

In her book *Radioactivity: A History of a Mysterious Science*, Marjorie C. Malley discusses the science and history of radioactivity:

> *Radioactivity burst into the world without warning. No precursors foreshadowed it, and nothing in nineteenth-century physics could have predicted it. Barely noticed at first, within a few years radioactivity became a prime topic for researchers. For the public radioactivity transformed from a minor curiosity into a potential font of miracles.*
>
> *The 1896 discovery of invisible uranium rays dramatically changed physics and chemistry as well as the lives of future generations. Fields as diverse as geology, archaeology, biology, medicine, meteorology, philosophy, power generation, and warfare were altered by the new findings. Radioactivity revealed details of the structure of matter and provided tools for investigating it.*

Source: Marjorie C. Malley. Radioactivity: A History of a Mysterious Science. New York: Oxford UP, 2011. Print. xix.

What's the Big Idea?

Take a close look at this excerpt. What is Malley saying about the importance of radioactivity? Pick out two details she uses to make her point. How has radioactivity affected the world?

IMPORTANT DATES

1867
Maria Sklodowska is born in Warsaw, Poland, on November 7.

1891
Maria moves to Paris, France, and enrolls at the Sorbonne with the French version of her name, Marie.

1895
Marie marries Pierre Curie in July.

1903
Pierre and Marie receive the Nobel Prize in physics in December.

1903
Marie earns a doctorate in physics, becoming the first woman to obtain the degree in France.

1906
Pierre dies in a carriage accident.

1895

Wilhelm Röntgen discovers X-rays in November.

1896

Henri Becquerel discovers that uranium emits rays of energy.

1898

The Curies discover polonium in July and radium in December.

1914

Construction finishes on the Radium Institute, Marie's lab devoted to the study of radioactivity.

1914–1918

Marie creates and heads the Red Cross's Radiology Service during World War I, which uses X-rays to help treat wounded soldiers.

1934

Marie dies on July 4.

STOP AND THINK

Tell the Tale

Chapter Five of this book discusses Marie's use of X-rays on the front lines of World War I. Write 200 words about carrying out this work. Describe the sights and sounds of the battle happening around her. What would it have been like to X-ray soldiers in battle? Be sure to set the scene, develop a sequence of events, and offer a conclusion.

Another View

This book has a lot of information about Marie Curie. As you know, every source is different. Ask a librarian or another adult to help you find another source about this renowned scientist. Write a short essay comparing and contrasting the new source's point of view with that of this book's author. What is the point of view of each author? How are they similar and why? How are they different and why?

You Are There

This book discusses Marie Curie's experience as a female scientist at the Royal Society. Imagine you are one of Marie's colleagues at that time. How would you feel seeing your fellow scientist excluded from giving public lectures?

Take a Stand

This book discusses Marie Curie's work on radioactivity. Do you think the use of radioactivity has improved the world? Or has it hurt more than it has helped? Write a brief essay explaining your opinion. Be sure to give reasons for your point of view. Include facts and details to support your reasons.

GLOSSARY

cataract
an ailment of the eye in which the lens gets cloudy

chemistry
the study of what things are made of, how they behave physically, and the forms they take

governess
a woman whose job is to care for and teach children in their home

matter
the material that makes up physical objects and takes up physical space

mineral
material that forms naturally underground, such as salt or pitchblende

Nobel Prize
a yearly award given to people who complete important work in chemistry, economics, literature, medicine, peace, or physics

nuclear
involving the nucleus of an atom

particles
tiny pieces of matter

LEARN MORE

Books

Krieg, Katherine. *Marie Curie: Physics and Chemistry Pioneer*. Minneapolis, MN: Abdo Publishing, 2014.

Steele, Philip. *Marie Curie: The Woman Who Changed the Course of Science*. Washington, DC: National Geographic Children's Books, 2007.

Websites

To learn more about Great Moments in Science, visit **booklinks.abdopublishing.com**. These links are routinely monitored and updated to provide the most current information available.

Visit **mycorelibrary.com** for free additional tools for teachers and students.

INDEX

ABOUT THE AUTHOR

Rebecca Rowell has put her degree in publishing and writing to work as an editor and as an author. Recent topics as author include Sylvia Earle, ancient India, and the US Marine Corps. She lives in Minneapolis, Minnesota.